Matthew Hale Carpenter

Speech of Matt Hale Carpenter

Matthew Hale Carpenter

Speech of Matt Hale Carpenter

ISBN/EAN: 9783337374990

Printed in Europe, USA, Canada, Australia, Japan

Cover: Foto ©Suzi / pixelio.de

More available books at **www.hansebooks.com**

SPEECH

OF

MATT H. CARPEN[TER]

...ation of the Memorial

College,

JULY, 1869.

— • —

and the Future Foreign Po[licy of]

the United States.

— • —

MILWAUKEE:

J. H. YEWDALE, BOOK AND JOB PRINTER, COR. EAST WATER AND HURON STS.

1869.

Mr. President, Ladies and Gentlemen:

The American people have just emerged from the thick darkness of national distresses : emerged, as no other nation could reasonably have expected to, from *such* dangers, triumphant, though bleeding at every pore. The first impulse of a great people on being delivered from eminent perils, is that of joy and thanksgiving ; then comes gratitude for those by whose guidance, under God, safety has been attained ; then a sad reflection upon the fearful sacrifices by which success has been purchased, and a tender recollection of those who have fallen in the strife ; and finally the composed mind gathers up the teachings of such a fearful experience :—wisdom for the guidance of future years. On the surrender of Lee and Johnson in 1865, our people gave themselves up to the wildest rejoicings ; for a time the toils, the trials, the sufferings of four dreadful years were all forgotten ; business places were closed, our people rushed out of doors, impromptu processions filled the streets ; music led our exultant emotions as far as musical sounds could conduct them ; and then the roar of cannon and the shoutings of the multitude took up the joyful strain and bore it in tumult to the skies. Our people are fond of excitement, and may be aroused to enthusiasm upon slight provocation. But *then* the grounds for national rejoicing were adequate and philosophical. Such dangers as had never threatened any government, had been averted ; such a rebellion as the world had never seen had been suppressed ; such results as had never before been accomplished by war, had been achieved. We plunged into the war cursed with the institution of slavery, three millions of our fellow creatures held in bitter bondage ; we came forth a nation of free men, equal in civil rights, no longer recognizing any distinctions of caste or color. Our young republic had successfully ended the experiment of its existence, and for the first time took its place—a full, round, high place,—among the powers of the earth. We had to thank God, after the storms of war had passed, that we at last possessed, what our fathers had hoped and prayed for, *" a country, and that a free country."*

Our people have shown their gratitude to their leaders in works more substantial than words. They have raised Grant above the army to the chair of Washington. Sherman they have made their chief captain ; an appointment for life with annual salary second only to that of the President. Sheridan they have made the worthy lieutenant of such a captain ; and others have been rewarded, and are still to be honored, according to their great merits. The widows and orphans of the war have been generously provided for. Everything that could be, has been done, to smooth the scars of a frightful struggle.

We have demonstrated that a great people know how to be both just and generous.

And now, four years after the war, and after the immediate and pressing demands upon us have been fully satisfied towards those who survived and came back to us from the battle field—we have come, in the midst of profound peace and general prosperity, in this beautiful day of teeming summer, to show our reverence for those *who came not back from the war ;* and to dedicate to their memory the beautiful hall which you have erected, monumental in form, and useful in fact ; thus uniting the memory of the departed with one of the great facilities for acquiring knowledge, a college library.

Pericles delivered his great oration, which Thucydides has preserved for us, one of the grandest specimens of ancient art, standing by the unburied remains of those who had fallen on the field, and surrounded by weeping mourners whose anguish had not yet been soothed by the healing power of time. Nevertheless, by far the greater part of that oration, is devoted to an examination of the character of Athenian institutions, to show that those who had fallen for Athens had not died for a vain or useless thing. We stand here to-day not in the freshness of individual grief; not to pay the last sad offices of respect to the outward material forms of those we have loved. Over their graves the green grass is waving and tropical flowers are cheerfully blossoming. Time has dried our tears and composed our

4

emotions. The sister comes not to weep for the brother; the father comes not to bend over the ghastly remains of his first born, not yet committed to sepulture. But we come as American citizens to thank God that in our deepest need the patriotism of our people was equal to the hour; we come to reflect rather than to weep; we come to gather up the lessons taught by their example; to consider the fruits of the victory they have secured for us, and hence to deduce our duty as a nation in the great future which opens before us with immortal splendor.

You have just been addressed by Professor Emerson, specially upon the character and services of those whose names are to be engraved upon the tablet of honor in this memorial hall. He knew them personally, loved them well, and has spoken of them with the tenderness befitting his theme, and an earnest eloquence becoming to himself. I shall therefore devote the short time allotted to me to a consideration of the character of our government and its duty in the immediate future.

God never made a man for the sake of making him; nor that he might amass wealth and corrupt himself with its enjoyment. Every man is sent into the world with certain qualities to be cultivated and developed; charged with duties to be performed, and clothed with responsibilities commensurate with his power; sent into the world that some other may be better for his having lived. So with nations; they grow up not for themselves alone; they are ordained of God ; they are the instrumentalities by which God accomplishes his purposes towards the human race. They who study human history, they who believe in the Gospels of Christ—*believe that the very hairs of our head are numbered and that not a sparrow falls without His notice*—cannot doubt that Empires come and go, and States are born and perish, in obedience to His sovereign will. Assuming that God is the founder of nations, that they are protected by His power, continued for His ends, and discontinued when they are no longer servicable,—either because their mission has been accomplished, or they have shown themselves unfit to accomplish it, and have thus become *cumberers of the ground*,—we may take up the history of any nation and reverently study the purpose for which God created it. Take for instance the Israelitish nation; consider it in the light of its surrounding conditions, study the principles which were given for its guidance ; read the solemn warning of Moses in that great farewell address before they crossed the Jordan :

" Beware that thou forget not the law of thy God,
" in not keeping his commandments, and his judgments,
' and his statutes, which I command thee this day ;
" lest when thou has eaten and art full, and hast
" built goodly houses and dwelt therein ; and when
" thy herds and thy flocks multiply, and thy silver
" and thy gold is multiplied, and all that thou hast
" is multiplied ; then thy heart be lifted up *and thou
"forget the Lord thy God*, which brought thee forth

" out of the land of Egypt, from the house of bondage,
" * * * and thou say in thine heart, *my power*
" and the might of mine hand hath gotten me this
" wealth ; * * and it shall be, if thou do at all
"· forget the Lord thy God, *and walk after other Gods,*
" *and serve them,* I testify against you this day that
" ye shall surely perish : as the nations which the
"· Lord destroyeth before your face so shall ye perish ;
" *because* ye would not be obedient unto the voice of
" the Lord your God;" Then study the subsequent
history of that nation, its prosperity in obedience,
its utter destruction when obedience ceased ; and it
would be neither rash nor irreverent to conclude that
God created that nation to preserve the knowledge
and the worship of the one true God, amid the
idolatry of surrounding nations ; and that He destroyed it, because it had ceased to perform the duty
for which it had been called into existance; ceased to
breathe the Spirit that God had breathed into it at
its birth. Its internal structure might be changed
to suit changing circumstances ; it might be ruled
by one law-giver like Moses, or by Judges or
Kings ; all *that* was immaterial ; but the essential
condition of its prosperity, nay of its existence as a
nation, was the worship of one God ; and when this
condition failed, the nation died.

So we might take up the history of Greece or of
Rome, and by studying what part it performed in the
advancement of man's civilization, the circumstances
under which it prospered, and the conditions under

which it declined as a nation, and thus deduce the purpose of God in establishing it as a nation. To such a method of examining the character of our government I desire to turn your thoughts ; not to its non-essential features, the structure of its framework, the division of its powers, or the excellency of its internal adaptation ; but to its spirit, its heaven imposed duty, the conditions under which it may hope to prosper, the dereliction under which it may apprehend the frown of God.

Human liberty is the essential condition of utmost human development. The child must be governed, disciplined, encouraged and restrained, by the parent ; all this tends to develop him into manhood. But there comes a time when he must be left free to act, free to think, free, so far as power is concerned, to chose between good and evil. So with the race ; the authority of kings and the superintendence of a priesthood may aid its infancy ; but there comes a stage of development in which *freedom* is the only condition of higher attainments. Many a child dies never knowing the independence of manhood ; many a nation has disappeared, and others will disappear, cursed to the last by the tyrany of kings and priests.

The *wise men* came from the East; they journeyed towards the West. Starting from utter darkness of absolute despotism in the East, and coming Westward, the dawn brightens and the day shines. On the utmost verge of Europe, a

8

little removed *from* Europe, an island in the Atlantic, England had advanced, in the seventeenth century, as far towards liberty as was consistent with the structure of her government. With a feudal foundation, a king and an aristocracy, she had reached vantage ground in the march ; had secured many of the blessings and some of the rights of a free people. The British monarchy had been the Moses of the nations; she had led the race in sight of the promised land, but now she was begining to wane.

Further advance she could not make under her form of government ; and her time for revolution had not yet arrived The power of the monarchy was great, the aristocracy were numerous and powerful, the republican element was small, the spirit of liberty and equality though growing, was still weak.   A little band of patriots, of ˉod fearing men, lovers of liberty because lovers of God, too few to stand upright in England, too resolute of purpose to submit to tyranny, turned their steps , still westward, and in mid winter planted the empire of freedom upon this *then* unpromising continent. It is quite unnecessary, for you are as familiar with it as I am, and time would fail me, to dwell upon the details of that settlement, and the settlement of other colonies upon these shores.   I only refer to it, to ask you ; who protected them, from famine, from dissensions internal, from dangers external, from the inclemency of the elements, and the hostility of

savages ? Who gave them the courage and inspired
them with the faith equal to their great task ? Turn
over in your own minds for I have no time even to
refer to the strange incidents in their wonderful history, verifying our belief that God superintends the
founding of states ; follow the colonies through their
infancy, down to the commencement of the revolution which ultimately separated them from the
parent state and made us an independant nation,
and then say; do you believe God had no part no design in all those wonderful events ? He saw the end
from the begining ; and the begining would not have
been if the end had not been intended. It is true
that the love of liberty in their hearts, the tyranny
of their king, their fleeing to these shores, their
founding of a free commonwealth, their growth to
power as a people, were all natural events. No
supernatural intervention attests God's purp ɔ in
their case. No thunders rolled down the mountains,
no summer led them over the wintry sea, no law of
nature was reversed for their aid or protection. If
we were about to send a colony to take possession of
a distant continent, we should make great display
about it ; have long processions and longer orations.
When we send an Envoy Extraordinary to a fɔ ʒign
power we send him in a government vessel, we land
him from beneath the star spangled flag, and amid
the roar of cannon to notify our foreign neighbor
that the *United States* has sent him to her shores.

But God's "ways are not as our ways, nor his thoughts our thoughts." He "speaks in his works." Jesus came an Envoy from heaven to earth, not in the glory which he had with his father before the world was ; not by angels attended through the opening heavens ; but he came not the less directly from the Father.

* *   * *   * *

On the 4th of July, 1776, our fathers met in solemn council, and promulgated to the world the principles which were to be our chart as a nation, and assumed a place among the nations of the earth. To that event and that day we refer our birth as a nation. Let us consider for a moment the great distinguishing principle upon which our institutions were based. We boast that that was the commencement of a new order of political things. Let us see for a moment in what that declaration differed from prior fundamental articles of political and governmental faith.

The brotherhood of man, the absolutely equal rights of all men, the right of all to participate in the privileges and benefits of civil government, as they share its burdens, although to our minds familiar and self evident truths, have dawned gradually upon the world, and made their way slowly into creeds of men. The Jew denied to every one not a Jew, not only the rights of citizenship in temporalities, but all hope of enjoying the blessings of heaven. The gentile might indeed be adopted into the Jewish commonwealth, but as a gentile he was nobody. When Pericles boasted that in Athens all men enjoyed equal privileges, and were preferred for their merits and not for their birth, he spoke in a city of which no inconsiderable portion of its inhabitants were sl.ves. By *all men* he meant all Athenians ; he did not recognize that any but Athenians were men. Jesus first burst the bonds of national selfishness. He came to establish a kingdom that should know no end, be united with the destinies of no nation, which should survive all and supercede all ; and its foundations were laid broadly accordingly. The Jew, the Gentile, the Scythian, the Barbarian, the Bond, the Free, the Black and the White, were invited to equal benefits in His Kingdom. He first taught principles broad enough to include all nations, races and colors in a common benefit. The declaration of our independence, the corner stone of our nationality, was mans first attempt to introduce the liberality of christian principle into the frame work of civil government ; it was a declaration—not that all Americans, all Englishmen, all Frenchmen were equal—but that *all men* were equal ; no matter where born, no matter whether learned or ignorant, rich or poor, black or white. It deduced the right to equality before the law, the right to participate in civil government, not from the accident of birth or condition, nor yet from race or color, *but from the fact of manhood alone.* Upon this principle, as the one great faith of our people, the ideal we intended to realize, the consummation we pledged ourselves to the accomplishment of, our fathers appealed to the God of battles, and succeeded. A more solemn covenant was never entered into between a nation and the God of nations. Upon that principle we stood through eight years of bloody war against one of the most powerful nations on the earth. Without an army, without a navy, without an exchequer, we stood, and withstood all the power of England, because truth will always stand, and right triumph over wrong, while God sits on the throne of the universe.

But after war had established our right to self government, and we came to fashion a government, this principle was not fully carried out. Slavery existed as a fact; and our fathers temporized with the condition of things. In the constitution they virtually secured the slave trade until 1808, and substantially guaranteed slavery in the states, until the states should abolish it. It is due to our fathers, however, to say that they expected slavery would soon be abolished by the states. No man who signed the constitution expected slavery would survive thirty years. But,—and perhaps to show the sad consequence of ever compromising with evil,—the event did not realize the expectation. The introduction of the cotton plant made slavery profitable; and gilded vice too often finds favor. The South first excused, then justified, then clamored for the extension of slavery; and down to the commencement of the rebellion in 1861, no man could see how the nation could purge itself of this monstrous sin. By civil means it could not. The constitution had put it out of the power of the nation, by committing it to the states where slavery existed; and those states would not abolish it. Our statesmen in 1850, resolved to cure the evil by wholly ignoring its existence. They solemnly resolved that the subject should never again be alluded to in or out of congress. That all agitation should cease. This was securing to the country peace according to the wisdom of time serving politicians ; but their wisdom was quite different from "the wisdom that is from above [which] is *first pure*, then peaceable." The so called "compromise measures" of 1850 were designed to secure peace ; but they were a solemn prediction of war. From that moment it was evident that no peaceful measures would be adopted to redress the great wrong of three millions of our people ; and *then* it became evident also, that the whole country must soon become slave country or free country. And after ten years of preparation on the part of the South and of criminal inactivity on the part of the North, the two sections drew the sword to determine the question of liberty or slavery for all the states ; and during four bloody, dismal years, "hope and fear did arbitrate the event." Grievously had we sinned and grievously did we answer it. Army after army rushed to the conflict ; hundreds after hundreds were laid in their graves ;

the land was baptised with blood. It was in this strife that your companions, whom to-day you honor, went forth with faith in their hearts, prayers on their lips, and the sword in their hand to stand and to fall for truth, for justice, for liberty and for God. Often in the darkness of those fearful years our sight failed us ; we could see no light ; but our people stood up strong in faith that God ruled the universe, and that our cause was safe. This faith carried us through the gloom. And finally in God's good time we emerged into the light of a triumphent and honorable peace. In this war our people expiated the sin of slavery and then the curse was withdrawn. And our nation stands to-day regenerated and renewed ; won by fearful evidences back to its first love,—*universal liberty.* Now for the first time in the history of our nation it is true as a fact, what our fathers announced as a theory, *that all men are created equal.* Now our re-constructed Union takes its place among the nations, the standard bearer and the champion of the rights of man. Our infancy is over ; our pupilage past, our manhood attained. We are no longer to flee from city to city to escape observation, no longer to bid men not to mention our works, no longer to feed on the wild figs of Bethany ; we have come into our own kingdom, and are ready to make up our jewels.

Let me pause in thought one moment at the close of the late war, and asking you to recall your emotions as the war progressed, your doubts, your fears, the

magnitude of the conflict, the bitterness of our ene-
mies, the unfriendly attitude of foreign nations, all
the obstacles overcome, the dangers past ; then let
me ask if you do not believe that the hand of God
in an especial manner led us through this sea of
troubles to the dry land of peace? If you believe your
bible you do believe that God interfered by special
providences, to secure the deliverence of the children
of Israel, from the land of Egypt. Turn to that history once more, and read again of the successive
plagues that fell like so many blows upon the heart
of Egypt, before she would consent that her slaves
might go forth. Then consider the similar conduct
of the south ; how without war, slavery would have
been continued ; how long after the war had begun,
the south might have laid down their arms and kept
the slaves ; how after the war was ended, the south
might have determined the question of negro suff-
rage ; and how by repeated obduracy amounting to
absolute stupidity, the south has forced the government to free the slaves and finally raise them to the
full enjoyment of legal and political rights ; then let
me ask : *do you see no parallel ?*

Another coincidence, and I will leave this part of
the subject. It would be interesting to consider,
but time forbids, the analogies that run through the
universe moral and material ; and to point out how
strangely, if it is mere accident, similar things, though
age distant in point of time, are similarly sur-
sounded.

Jesus was " a man of sorrows and acquainted with grief." His public ministry was one of toil and trial. He was bearing the worlds burdens, touched at its sorrows, and suffering for its sins. We read of him walking up the mountain, walking on the waters, agonizing in prayer, and weeping at the grave of him whom he loved. On one occasion, and on one only, He employed the semblance of a triumph. Once he *rode* into Jerusalem ; rode over a way sprinkled with the garments of his disciples and the green branches of Judean palms ; rode in triumph, amid the shoutings of the multitude ; " *Hosanna to the son of David.*" The day upon which this event transpired is celebrated by the church, and for designation it is styled "Palm Sunday." On the next Friday—"Good Friday," Jesus gave up his life, and was laid in the tomb.

I am not appealing to any superstitious feeling, nor drawing any irreverent comparison ; merely noting a remarkable co-incidence. President Lincoln took the helm of state amid the storms of war. For four years he suffered the anguish his situation imposed, he mourned with the mourners, he wept and prayed for the deliverance of his people. But finally, on a bright Sabbath morning in April, 1865, Lee surrendered the rebel hosts to Lincoln's captain and the war was ended. The news flew on the wires all over the land. That was a day of national rejoicing. None of us will ever forget it. On that day the clergy ministered in the usual way, at the altar.

And old deacons, accustomed by life long discipline never to turn their backs upon the "illuminated temple of the Lord," remained to attend the morning and evening sacrifices as usual. But where were the people? In the streets wild with excitement of joy. There are times when the Christian heart is too full for mere utterance ; times when the roar of cannon and the shoutings of the multitude are as genuine,—may they not be as acceptable,—praise as the chanted psalm or the whispered prayer. So Miriam went forth, celebrating the deliverance from the Red sea, and led the women of Israel with timbrels and dances, chanting that immortal song of human exultation, " Sing ye to the Lord, for He hath " triumphed gloriously ; the horse and his rider hath " He thrown into the sea. "

This first happy day of President Lincoln's official life, the first happy day of our people for four long years, chanced to fall on the "Palm Sunday" of 1865. The next Friday—" Good Friday "—Lincoln was shot. Mere coincident ; mere accident ; yes ; but human history is full of such suggestive accidents.

In passing from our first proposition, that God has established this nation, watched over it in an espicial manner, and protected it by special providences ; it is encouraging to think that such is the belief of our people. It crops out every where ; from the pulpit, in the press, in the speeches of our public men, in the conversation of our people. All speak the language of hope, of young ardent hope, and faith in God's superintending providence. In no other nation is this so eminently true. Look at the condition of old England to-day, and read the suggestive debates in the House of Lords on the Irish church bill. The Lords speak as though they were oppressed with the belief that there is no future for the monarchy. England stands to-day in the decrepitude of age, folding about her the shabby robes of worn out custom ; "perplexed with the fear of change ;" unable to advance ; unable to suppress the influences which are advancing step by step to throw open the temple of exclusive and heriditary privilege to the admission of the profane populace. "The voice of the people," when it utters the settled faith of a nation, " is the voice of God."

* *   * *   * *

And now, in the firm belief that God in his providence established this nation for a purpose,—to stand as a bulwork among the nations for the protection of the rights of man—,that it will prosper in proportion as it is true to the purpose of its institution, and will cease to be, whenever it no longer performs its duty ; that its manhood is attained, and its time for action arrived, it remains to enquire, *what can we do in the interest of universal liberty ?*

With a nation, its field of labor, *is the world.* The civilized powers of the earth in the society of nations, stand in much the same relation to each other, that individuals hold towards each other in civil society ; and their intercourse is regulated by the law of nations, which Montesque says is, "founded on "the principle, that different nations ought to do "each other as much good in peace, and as little "harm in war, as possible, without injury to their "true interests ;" and we may add, without injury to the true interests of mankind. Nations are equal in rights, and wholly independent of each other. And every nation has an absolute right, as regards its neighbors, to establish such form of civil polity as it pleases. If any people prefer a Republican or a monarchial government they are entitled to have it ; and no other nation has the right to interfere. This is the undoubted doctrine of the Law of Nations ; and every nation is bound to observe it ; and any nation which violates it, gives cause of offence to every other nation ; because each is interested that this law should be observed by all. This law then, is our law, both in its restraints and in its privileges. All that we do as a nation must be done in obedience to its provisions ; and we have an undoubted right to require of all other nations the same obedience. Any intervention on our part to coerce the establishment of republican institutions in Spain, would be an infraction of this law ; and any intervention by England or France to establish monarchy over that people would be equally unlawful.

We have said that our field is the world ; let us

look over this field, and see if there is ought that
we can do.   .

England is the first country we meet, surveying
the field eastward, and her present condition and
the relations which exist between that government
and ours, merit a more extended consideration than
the time will warrant. The first thing to be exam-
ined there, because at present it is engrossing all
her thought, is the contest hourly growing hotter
and hotter between the people and the privileged
classes. In form she has a monarchial government;
a queen ; a house of Lords representing the nobility,
the landed aristocracy, and the Established church
of the realm ; and a house of commons standing for
the people. The house of commons is overwhelm-
ingly republican; the house of Lords is as thorough-
ly wedded to existing abuses in church and state ;
the houses are engaged in a fierce struggle for
supremacy ; and the queen is a silent and powerless
observer of the contest. The commons have passed
a bill disestablishing the Irish church ; the Lords
after the most violent and disorderly debate ever
known in that house,—a debate during which by-
standers for the first time in English history groaned
at the nonsense of a Lord—destroyed the effect of
the bill by amendments, which the commons have
indignantly rejected. The difference between the
houses is one of principle which no committee of
conference can reconcile, and one house or the
other, must recede ; and it is certain that the com-

mons will not, because they are supported by the people ; and the voice of the people is omnipotent even in Great Britain. This bill may be delayed, it cannot be defeated. When it becomes a law, there is no principle upon which the establishment of the English church can be defended, and it must go with the Irish church. Then the Bishops must leave the house of Lords; and then the House of Lords, purged of its only popular element, may well apprehend the accidents which John Bright threatened them with ; and the crown itself will be in equal danger. Revolutions in popular feeling never go backwards The movements in England at the present time, give goodly promise that at no distant day Great Britain will be a republic in form as it already is in substance. At all events it is safe to predict that the people of England will hereafter control the government whatever may be its form.

The condition of our relations with that government enables us either to aid or embarrass the liberal party in England, without any violation of the law of nations. During the late war, that government was in the hands of the tory party ; and the aristocracy of England sympathized as was to have been expected, with the slave holding aristocracy of the south. The pirate ship Alabama, was built in full view of the government ; its intended use was well known ; it was manned with English Seaman, and was in all respects, except its commander, an

English vessel. It went forth to prey upon our commerce, in the interest of a slave-holder's rebellion. The actual damage to our shipping and merchandise, as shown by claims filed in the office of the Secretary of State, amounts, it is said, to nine millions three hundred thousand dollars, in round numbers ; a large sum certainly, but still a sum that we can save by economical administration, before breakfast. This sum is capable of exact 'liquidation, and must be paid in money, whether England remains a monarchy or becomes a republic. But we may suit the time and manner of enforcing this claim to circumstances ; and thereby may indirectly exert a powerful influence upon English politics. Our government may pay these claims to our citizens ; and charge the amount in the great ledger of national accountability ; to be collected when we please, and as we please; through the slow methods of diplomacy, or by the quick, sharp. process of reprisal and war. This acknowledged claim against England, in the hands of our government, is worth more than its face, and is the most effectual bond we could hold against England to keep the peace.

But this claim is only a drop in the bucket, of the great injury committed by England upon American interests, the rights of man, and the cause of liberty, during the war. She lost no opportunity to increase our difficulties, to prolong the war, to ensure the utter destruction of this great and much envied republic. She furnished rebels with arms and money, she gave countenance to their presumption, and encouragement to their wickedness, in every possible way. The injuries committed by the Alabama fell upon our material interests and may be repaired by time and industry. But our pecuniary injuries do not measure the transgressions of England. Hers was a crime against humanity and the moral sense of the world. It is incapable of computation in figures; it cannot be paid in money. Nor should we by accepting money for this injury, say to the world, that we are a nation of pedlers; that we look only to cash balances; that any foreign nation is at liberty to fire upon our flag, insult our sovereignty, wring our noses, *and send us a check*

The insolence of England in the matter of Mason and Slidell, was even more insupportable than the injuries she committed by the Alabama. They were on their way to Europe in a British vessel, one the accredited representative of the rebellion to the court of Victoria, and the other to the court of Napoleon. An American naval officer boarded the vessel, and arrested these ministers plenipotentiary of treason, and lodged them safely in a military stronghold of our government. Conceding this proceeding to have been irregular, and technically a violation of the rights of a neutral power, yet what an admirable opportunity it afforded England to show a friendly feeling towards our government. We were in a hand to hand struggle for our national existence. England was at profound peace with all the world. Years might have been employed by that fat and lazy old monarchy in investigations, in asking from our government the circumstances of the case, and thus giving us an opportunity to release these traitors, if they must be released, without suffering any humiliation. In 1837, when Canada was in revolt, the ship Caroline, was, or was supposed to be aiding the Canadian patriots. A British force invaded our territory, cut her loose from her moorings in American waters, and sent her a riven monument of British wrath, blazing over the cataract of Niagara, freighted with the dead body of at least one American citizen. A clearer case of the actual invasion of a neutral power, a more wanton violation of the law of nations, never was seen. Yet this offense was suffered by our government to go for four years through the easy stages of diplomacy, and it was finally settled in the correspondence which led to the Webster-Ashburton treaty, by Ashburton's saying he was sorry, and Webster's saying that would do. But our friendly forbearance was not followed by England in the case of Mason and Slidell. Upon the exparte reports of her own subjects, England decided the case in her own favor, and sent us a peremptory demand for an apology and for the immediate release of the traitors. Three days afterwards, the French government evidently at the instigation of England, directed the French minister at Washington to inform our government how deeply aggrieved France was at the outrage we had committed upon England. This combination of two great nations was intended to overawe and browbeat our government, and I never can think of Seward's reply to England's demand without feeling that the design completely succeeded. That reply, in seventeen solid pages, more or less, is the most uncandid and shameful paper that ever emenated from an American Secretary of State. It asserted (1) that we had a perfect right to take these rebels; (2) that we had no right whatever to take them ; (3) that we were agoing to give them up ; and (4) that we would not do so if it were of any consequence to detain them. After determining to release these prisoners Seward's reply should have been couched in ten lines. He should have informed England that her demand was technically right, and was acceded to because it was right ; and that the direct manner and curt style in which she had made her demand would be the precedent we should follow in demanding our rights of England in the future.

For all these injuries and all this insolence, we have a right to hold England responsible, as one nation must answer to another ; we have a perfect right to go to war with her if we please ; and this right will keep. We can bide our time ; select the occasion ; and if in some crises of her political destiny we should see that it was in our power, by enforcing our utmost rights by war, to be an instrument in the hands of God to avenge the outrages committed by that blood-stained monarchy, and in establishing the preponderance of the republican element of her people; no principle of the law of nations would be violated, that we had chosen that moment for the stern enforcement of our just rights.

One nation in dealing with another is at liberty to hold the whole nation responsible for the wrongs committed by the governing class of the offending nation. But a generous and powerful nation is not bound to enforce its just demands unless it pleases to do so; and will not, whenever it can see that the injury to be inflicted by war would fall upon guiltless heads. And we ought not to ignore the fact that, although the aristocracy of England, which happened at that time to be the government, were most unfriendly to us, the people of England *were our friends*. There is not a grander instance of self-sacrificing devotion to principle in the history of the world, than was exhibited by the manufacturers of England in the sturdy resolution with which they stood up for the rights of our government, testifying their sympathy for our cause, in the midst of a population starving for want of employment. Cotton they could not obtain, without recognizing the independence of the South. Yet they elected to suffer whatever hardships might come to themselves rather than wink at so great a national crime; and they kept so keen a watch and so steady an eye upon their government that it dare not recognize

the South. A declaration of war at this time would
visit its losses and hardships, so far as England is
concerned, upon the very classes who were our warm
friends, and did and suffered everything they
could for our sake. The aristocracy of England
would not fight many battles, nor pay much in taxation. The people of England who were not at
fault, would thus be made to expiate the sins of their
rulers which they steadily protested against when
committed. This we do not desire. In a spirit of
generous statesmanship, let us rather say to our
brother republicans of England, "you have got the
aristocracy on a down grade, *now push them.* We
will wait for our ten millions, actual pecuniary loss,
until you get into power and can pay it ; and when
you have trampled the governing classes under your
heel, you will thereby have saved us the trouble
of chastising them for their insolence ; and then we
will clasp hands across the Atlantic in joint sympathy with every people struggling to be free."

The great offence of England, was an offence
against the world, an act of rebellion against
the moral government of God ; and we have no
right to take the place of, the Almighty and com-
pound her crimes for money. The wages of sin in
the individual is death. The wages of sin in the
case of a great nation, is destruction. And if it
shall please God, in His wisdom, to visit upon the
guilty old monarchy of England, the utmost penalty

28

of her high transgression, we at least can say " *Thy will be done.*"

It is time that the plain truth should be spoken ; and frankness though a little disagreeable, will tend to promote an adjustment of our differences with Great Britan. We are sick and tired of the conventional hypocrisy that has so long characterised the intercourse between the public men of both countries ; sick and tired of the everlasting songs that celebrate our *pretended* unity of race, language and institutions. The fact is that between the people of the United States and the people of England there may, and there does exist warm sympathy and sincere friendship. But between a growing hopeful people like ours, looking to the future, and rushing on in the path of improvement and reform and an old proud, expiring aristocracy clinging to the past and resisting all change, like that which has governed Great Britain, there is no friendship, there can be none. We have no opinions, no hopes, no ends in common. There is indeed one mutual *sentiment* ; they would rejoice over our downfall *as we certainly should at theirs.*

* * * * * *

I have devoted so much time to England, that the review of other parts of *our field* must necessarily be brief; but "good omens cheer us" from France, from Spain, from Italy and from all Europe. Napolean is purchasing a brief continuance of power by concessions to the people. Our morning papers tell

us that he has determined to grant the great boon
of the *responsibility of ministers.* This is the principle upon which the English nation has withstood
and advanced upon arbitrary power, until the Queen
is tied hand and foot, and must obey her parliament.
The experiment in France will ripen into fruits even
faster then it did in England. This concession
made and arbitrary power is dead in France.

Spain is rocking in the throes of revolution. Left
to herself she would be a republic within twelve
months. We have recently sent a minister to that
country to represent our opinions and sentiments.
There he will meet the representatives of England
and France. What is he to say to them? I know
nothing of his instructions ; and am therefore in no
danger of disclosing state secrets. But I know
what he *should* say to them, and have a pretty
clear idea of what, if left to himself,
he would say. Spain is to-day, if the opportunity be properly improved, the most important
of all our missions. Her affairs are in that forma-
tion state, where the proper course pursued by the
representative of this great republic may contribute
much to make her a republic; and that too without
violating the law of nations. The time has passed
in the history of the world, when nothing but force
can avail in shaping the course of public events.
Our minister will find in Spain a great republican
party, the remnant of an aristocracy, and a people
generally ready to receive with great joy the gospel

30

of equal rights. It will be in his power, in various ways representing this great nation, to encourage and direct the republican tendencies of that people. And to the representatives of France and England, he should say : " this people have a perfect right to fashion their own institutions in their own way. The United States hope they will establish a Republic. Nevertheless, we do not propose to interfere in the matter beyond friendly advice ; because the law of nations, and the first principles of self government forbid. But the law of nations is our law as well as yours ; it binds you as well as us ; this law we will not violate, and you *shall not* violate this law." " Simply this and nothing more " and Spain will be a Republic. Regenerated by free institutions, by the correction of abuses, the distribution of rights and privileges, and by the impetus that liberty will give to the enterprise of her people, Spain may be once more what she once was a first class power ; and send forth influences potent for the reformation of the world, which will be of far greater moment to man, than all the discoveries made by her ancient mariners.

Italy too is hopeful ground for republicanism. Her people are arousing from the lethergy of centuries, and looking to nationality and freedom, once more ; and the march of liberal thought has reached even the masses of Prussia, Austria and Russia. Everything indicates an awakening, and an advance ;

and all changes hereafter, are likely to be in favor of the people, and against the privileged classes.

In this condition of the world the United States should and must have a foreign policy. It is shirking the responsibilities of our position, neglecting the duty God has cast upon us as a nation. to stand indifferent to the issue between Republican institutions and arbitrary power now going on all over the world. While slavery existed here, our representatives abroad were constrained to silence. They had to say to Russia and Austria, "you may trample upon Hungary, we are oppressing the negro ; say nothing to us and we will say nothing to you." But we have cast out this fearful beam from our own eye, and are now authorized, by divine license, to consider the mote in our brothers eye. We are no longer a house divided against itself ; talking freedom and upholding slavery, The liberation of our slaves has enfranchised the nation. We ought hereafter to speak earnestly, and need not apprehend the taunt: "Physician heal thyself." We must plant ourselves upon the principle of the law of nations, that every people have the right to govern themselves by such form of government as they please ; and that no other nation has a right to dictate upon the subject. But says some cautious soul, this means war, and war will result in taxation. Not so : it means peace ; peace, if we have to fight for it ; peace for ourselves and for all mankind. We say for instance that Spain has a right to become a Republic or a monarchy as she shall elect. But says the objector, after you have said so, suppose Napoleon sends an army into Spain to set up a monarchy, then you must make war upon France. Not necessarily. We should then say to France that she had violated the law of nations. and given all other nations offence. But it does not follow that we should make war upon France. When England sent a military force into our territory and captured the ship Caroline and sent it over the cataract, she gave us just cause for war. But we did not go to war with her. We treasured it up as an affront for which she must some time answer. And in due time the settlement came to our satisfaction. When England sent forth the Alabama to destroy our commerce, she gave us cause for war. We have not made war yet; and whether we ever shall will depend upon circumstances, and upon our own good pleasure. The assumption that war must follow if the United States objects to one nation's abusing and oppressing another, ignores the spirit of our age and the influences of our modern national intercourse. It has been said that God and one man constitute a majority. That is, one man, right, is stronger than all men wrong. A clear truth supported by one powerful nation, will soon be recognized by all nations. Napoleon said at St. Helena that Russia desired to deal with Turkey ; but that he would not consent that Russia should have Constantinople for that would give the dominion of Asia; and that Russia kept her hands

off. The protest of any first class power, against
the intervention of Russia in the Hungarian struggle, would probably have saved that nationality.
Hungary could have maintained her liberties against
Austria ; but eighty thousand bayonets from Russia
turned the scale and crushed out the nationality of
a liberty loving people. We have grown to such
importance as a nation, that we can no longer wink
at one nation's oppressing another, or stand by while
a wrong is committed which it is in our power to
prevent, without being responsible, morally, for that
wrong. But says the objector, Washington, in his
farewell address counselled us to avoid all entangle-
ment in the affairs of other nations : can any man
be sound who differs from our Father Washington?
The farewell address spake the words of wisdom for
his own generation, and correctly enunciated the
duty of our people at that time. We were then in
our infancy ; three or four millions of people scat-
tered over a wilderness of country, burthened with
a debt we could not pay ; and our interference in
European affairs under such circumstances would
have been as ridiculous as it would have been
ineffectual. It would have ruined us and benefited
nobody. No nation, no individual, is in duty
bound to attempt impossibilities. Washington was
addressing a people then in the nursery ; and said
in substance, "you are little boys; now be *good* little
boys, and every body will love you." Helplessness is
an immunity to a nation in its infancy, as to an in-

dividual child. But that condition has passed; that immunity has ceased. We have attained our manhood, and must now face the duties and bear the responsibilities of manhood. *We must be about our Fathers business.*

But says the objector, no matter if this is our duty; that will get us into a war, and increase taxation; we had better not notice the outrages which one foreign nation may inflict upon another. We may live in peace and prosperity, though Hungary be trampled in the dust; we may get very rich though despotism may violate all law in other places and extinguish every impulse or longing for liberty elsewhere

. Away with this philosophy of gain, this wisdom of the pedlar. If it is right for us to stand by and silently witness wrongs we might arrest; let us do so, because it is right, and not because it might cost money to do our duty. Everything is expensive; it costs time to pray; costs money to clothe your wives and educate your children; costs money to sustain civil government, to administer justice, to carry forward the methods of our complex civilization. And what was this vast continent, its accumulating population, its rich fields, its exhaustless mines, its facilities for commerce, its immeasurable and yet undeveloped resources of national wealth, given to us for? That we might become the richest and most corrupt nation on earth? Or have we received them from the Giver of all good, to use in his service and intrust for the benefit of our race? What would you say of an individual who reasoned thus selfishly. I see a thief breaking into my neighbor's house; shall I fold my arms and say nothing; I see a murderer pursuing my friend, shall I silently seek the shelter of my own house, lest by opposing the murderer I might get his ill will or his bad blows? You would pronounce me a *sneak*, the law would declare me an accessory, and punish me accordingly. The loss of honor, the neglect of duty, are greater calamities than war. Advance in the line of duty and God is our shield, who can harm us; turn aside from duty, men will despise us, and God will destroy us.

*　　*　　　*　　*　　　*　　*

The brave young men who went forth from this College to suppress the slaveholders attempt to re- verse the decree of God, and exalt slavery above liberty, sleep in bloody graves, yet live in our tender and our grateful remembrance. Their example ap- peals to our manhood and our conscience. They help- ed to carry our government through a crisis in its exis- tence; to establish it firmly upon immutable truth; and give it the grandest opportunity a nation ever had, to benefit mankind. It now devolves upon us who survive to determine whether their lives were laid down in vain. And in no way, I conceive, can we so truly honor them, as in studying well and per- forming faithfully the duty they have helped to cast upon us. If we prove equal to our opportunity, if we stand firmly for justice and for equality among men, if we keep the lamp of liberty trimmed and burning, and allow its light to shine from our altitude through out the world, we honor them; they have not died in vain; therefore it seems to be appropriate to this occasion to enquire into our new duties and gird ourselves for their performance.

They died for others, not for themselves ; and let us so live as to exert the influence of the exalted position they have conferred upon us for the welfare of mankind, and not for the attainment of selfish ends.